Ceremonies and Celebrations

WEDDINGS

LINDA SONNTAG

HODDER
Wayland

an imprint of Hodder Children's Books

Ceremonies and Celebrations
WEDDINGS

Other titles in this series are:

BIRTHS • FEASTS AND FASTING • GROWING UP
• LIFE'S END • PILGRIMAGES AND JOURNEYS

Produced for Hodder Wayland by
Roger Coote Publishing
Gissing's Farm, Fressingfield
Suffolk IP21 5SH, UK

Published in Great Britain in 2000 by Hodder Wayland, an imprint of
Hodder Children's Books

First published in paperback 2001

Editor: Alex Edmonds
Designer: Tim Mayer
Consultants
Khadijah Knight is a teacher and consultant on multicultural education
and Islam. She is also the author of several children's books about Islam.
Marcus Braybrooke is a parish priest and lecturer and writer on inter-
faith relations. He is joint President of the World Congress of Faiths.
Kanwaljit Kaur-Singh is a local authority inspector for education.
She has written many books on the Sikh tradition and appears on
television regularly.
Sharon Barron regularly visits schools to talk to children about Judaism.
She has written two books about Judaism for Hodder Wayland.
Meg St. Pierre is the Director of the Clear Vision Trust, a charitable
trust that aims to inform and educate about the teachings of Buddha.
VP Hemant Kanitkar is a retired teacher and author of many books
on Hinduism.

Picture Acknowledgements
Circa Picture Library 10 (Ged Murray), 11 (Barrie Searle), 12 (Ged
Murray), 28 (John Smith); Hutchison Picture Library *front cover* top
left, top right (Liba Taylor), bottom left, bottom right (Kerstin
Rodgers), 1, 4, 6, 8 (Robert Francis), 9 (Nancy Durrell McKenna), 13
(Liba Taylor), 14 (R. Aberman), 16, 19 (K. Rodgers), 21 (John Hatt),
22 (M. Macintyre), 26 (Liba Taylor), 29; Panos Pictures 5, 7, 15
(John Miles), 17 (Mark McEvoy), 18, 20 (Leo Dugust), 23 (Dean
Chapman), 24 (Paul Cluagle), 25 (Leo Dugust), 27 (Liba Taylor).

A Catalogue record for this book is available from the British
Library.
ISBN 0 7502 2817 2

Printed and bound in Italy by G. Canale & C.Sp.A

Hodder Children's Books
a division of Hodder Headline Limited
338 Euston Road, London NW1 3BH

CONTENTS

Why do People get Married?

For people of many faiths around the world, marriage is the foundation of life together and of the family. Two people marry to give each other love, friendship and support through bad and good times. Many couples hope for children and plan to bring them up in a secure and loving home, and perhaps to worship in the same faith as their parents. In this way, marriage becomes the cornerstone on which society is built.

People who are not religious often live together happily and have children. Some marry at a simple ceremony in a register office and others see no need for a public display of commitment. But for followers of the world's major faiths, it is often important to make their vows to each other in the eyes of their God. It takes a great deal of faith, as well as love, to get married, because relationships need to be worked at and are not always easy.

Wedding rings

Couples often exchange rings during the wedding ceremony. A ring symbolizes eternity, because it has no beginning and no end. It stands for the couple's love for one another. It also symbolises a bond. A ring on someone's finger means that he or she is committed to a partner.

The custom of throwing confetti, meaning 'sweets', over the bride and groom comes from Italy. There people used to throw little sweets over the couple to wish them good luck. ▶

So people marry in faith, hope and love, and the wedding day is a day of great rejoicing. To mark the importance of the occasion, friends and family often come from far and wide to bring gifts and good wishes, and share in the wedding feast. But there are many ways in which people of different faiths can solemnize their marriage and celebrate their wedding.

▼ *In many countries, couples celebrate their marriage by parading through the streets of the town or city with their guests. They may have their photographs taken in front of pretty parks or buildings, such as this cathedral in Russia.*

The Christian Tradition

Many Christian couples around the world still get married in 'traditional' style in a church, where they make a solemn promise to God to love and care for each other for all their lives. Today many people live together to make sure they get on well before they decide to marry. People who don't usually go to church can get married at a simple ceremony in a register office, and some may choose to have a private service, perhaps led by a friend, to seal their union.

▼ *The bride may have a party a few days before she is married to celebrate the end of her single life. Very often only female friends and relatives are invited to attend.*

Getting engaged

When a couple agree to marry, they sometimes get engaged. The man may give his partner an engagement ring as a symbol of his love, and she wears this on her wedding finger – the third finger of her left hand. If they are getting married in a Protestant church, the pair go to see the vicar, who explains the importance of the marriage vows. Banns may be called in church. This means that for three weeks running, the vicar asks the congregation if anyone knows of a reason why the couple may not marry.

Planning the wedding

▲ The wedding day is said to be the most important day of the couple's lives. Preparations for the event may take many months and the bride's dress is often designed and made especially for her.

The two families work hard to prepare for the wedding day. If the wedding is to be a big celebration, they send out invitations to relatives and friends, order a wedding cake and choose special food and clothes, music and flowers for the big day. If the bride and groom decide to have a private service, they may write their own promises and words of love and perhaps go to a restaurant with a few close friends after the service rather than have a big party.

Sacred text

'Love is always patient and kind. It envies no one. Love is never boastful or conceited. It is never rude or quick to take offence. Love does not keep score of wrongs. It does not gloat over other people's misfortunes but delights in the truth. There is nothing that love cannot face. There is no limit to its faith, its hope and its endurance. Love will never come to an end.'

The Bible: 1 Corinthians 13: 4–7

In church

The groom and his best man – a close friend who is entrusted with the smooth-running of the day – stand at the front of the church with all the guests in their seats. Then the music strikes up and the bride walks up the aisle. Most brides wear an ornate white or cream dress with a veil, to show modesty and purity. Traditionally the bride is accompanied up the aisle by her father, who will 'give her away'. This tradition dates back to when brides were handed over from the care of their family to the care of their husband. Sometimes the bride's mother or a friend does this instead. The bride may also have bridesmaids to hold the train of her dress and help and support her throughout the day.

▼ *Christian couples often choose to get married outdoors. This could be in a garden, on a beach or even on a remote hilltop.*

The service

The bride and groom stand before the altar to take their vows, which they repeat after the vicar. Often, they exchange rings. In the Greek Orthodox Church, red and gold crowns are put on their heads and they hold lighted candles. Everyone sings hymns, and there are readings from the Bible. The couple kneel before the altar for a blessing and finally they sign the register, which records them as legally married. As they leave the church, friends throw flower petals, rice or confetti over the couple for good luck.

◀ *The vicar witnesses the bride and groom signing the register, which is the final stage of the wedding ceremony.*

The party

The wedding feast – the first meal of the couple's married life – may take place in a hotel, at home, or in a marquee in the garden. There are speeches from the bride's father and the best man. Then the guests drink to the couple's future happiness. The wedding cake is ceremonially cut by the bride and groom to indicate the start of their lives together. Everyone celebrates with music and dancing.

The honeymoon

A honeymoon is a holiday that often begins married life. The couple leave the wedding party, sometimes in a car that their friends have secretly decorated with balloons, old tin cans and boots, for a secret destination. There they can be alone together and relax after the excitement of their wedding.

Rosie's story

'My name is Rosie. I was bridesmaid at my sister's wedding. I wore flowers in my hair and carried the bride's train, a long lace headdress that trailed behind her. The groom gave me a necklace as a souvenir of the day. As she left for her honeymoon, my sister threw her bouquet into the crowd of guests. I caught it and traditionally this means that I will get married next.'

The Jewish Tradition

In Jewish communities around the world, marriage partners are often found through large networks of family and friends. A man and a woman are introduced if they seem suited by character and lifestyle. Many happy marriages are made in this way, but in the end, it is always up to the individual to choose his or her partner.

Getting ready to marry

A Jewish wedding can happen on any day of the week except the Sabbath, which runs from sundown on Friday to sundown on Saturday. A few days before the wedding, the bride goes to purify herself in a special pool called the *mikveh*, taking with her her mother or a friend. Then, on the Sabbath before the ceremony, the groom visits the synagogue for a reading from the *Torah*, the scrolls of Jewish Law.

◄ *The groom prepares for the talk that he has to give before his wedding ceremony by reading the Torah. The guests are traditionally supposed to stop him from delivering his speech by making as much noise as possible or distracting him.*

The day arrives

The wedding day is a day of great happiness, but also time to ask for forgiveness for past sins and to make a fresh start. So the bride and groom may fast (eat nothing) until after the ceremony to symbolise cleansing the body. With covered heads, they stand under the *huppah* – a canopy held up by four poles – which represents the home the pair will make together. Its sides are open, to show the fragility of relationships, but also to indicate that they are part of the wider community, which is there to help them. The ceremony can take place in a synagogue, garden or park. Apart from the rabbi, there must be at least ten adult males present (the *minyan*). Everyone faces the *Ark*, a chest containing the *Torah*, on the east side of the synagogue.

▶ Traditionally, the poles at the four corners of the huppah were held up by four people from the wedding party. Some couples don't have a huppah, but stand under a shawl.

▲ *The custom of unveiling the bride to identify her,* bedecken, *comes from the story from the Bible in which Jacob married Rachel by mistake, instead of Leah, the woman he loved.*

Bedecken

In a ceremony called *bedecken*, the groom lifts the bride's veil to identify her. The rabbi gives a blessing over a cup of wine, and the groom and bride drink from it. Then the groom puts the wedding ring on the bride's right index finger. He vows to feed, clothe and care for her.

The breaking of the glass

The seven blessings are sung or recited, and the bride and groom again drink wine from the same glass, to show that they will share all things. The seven blessings praise God for creating the human race and bringing joy and gladness into the world. The groom then dashes the glass to the floor and grinds it underfoot. Some say this is a reminder of the destruction of the temple in Jerusalem, others that it symbolizes the fragility of happiness. Friends sometimes call out, '*Mazel tov!*' (good luck!) at this point.

Quiet togetherness

The groom and bride sign a covenant (contract) of marriage, and then they are taken to a private room. Here they spend a short while alone together and share a bowl of soup to break their fast, before rejoining their guests. They have a busy time ahead, as in traditional communities there is a whole week of celebrations. The couple will be guests of honour in a different home every night, with the seven blessings repeated after each meal.

Sacred text

These sayings from the Jewish books of law, show that many Jews believe that individual people cannot develop fully until they unite in marriage.

'A man without a wife is incomplete.'

'All the blessings that a man receives come to him only in the merit of his wife.'

The Talmud

▼ *After the wedding, the guests dance to celebrate the union of the two people.*

The Muslim Tradition

When a young Muslim is ready to marry, his or her family may make enquiries among friends and relations, and even over the Internet through well-regulated Islamic matchmaking websites, to find a suitable partner. The young people are free to accept or reject the candidates suggested by their family. In the end, they make the choice.

A legal contract

▼ In Turkey, Muslims get together to sing and dance at a traditional ceremony before the wedding.

The Prophet Muhammad (pbuh) taught that marriage was blessed by Allah. But the marriage ceremony is not a religious one. Each Muslim couple makes their own legal contract, setting out the rules for their marriage. In a Muslim marriage, the husband must promise to look after and provide for his wife, even if she is wealthy. She keeps whatever she owns before they marry, and in addition her husband gives her a gift of money or property.

The patterns painted on the bride's hands and feet symbolize the strength of love between a couple. ▶

Henna Night

Once they have agreed to marry, the bride and groom may exchange gold rings with their names engraved on them at the engagement party. Then every night for about a week before the wedding, it is traditional for the couple, each in their separate homes, to get together with friends to sing, play the drums and dance. On the night before the wedding – Henna Night – they each have their hands and feet painted in delicate patterns with *mehndi*, a paste made of the herb henna, which stains the skin dark red. This is a cultural, rather than religious, tradition that originates from Muslims who lived in India.

Zahra's story

'My name is Zahra and I live in Iran. When I first met my bridegroom, Hasan, we were led into a room from opposite doors and looked at each other in a mirror on the far wall. This is an old tradition – the mirror shows us how we will look in Paradise.'

At the wedding

Muslims may get married in a mosque, where the marriage is led by an *imam* (a leader of prayers in a mosque). But as the marriage is a contract rather than a religious ceremony, this is not necessary, and any Muslim man may marry the couple. The Qur'an says that a man can have up to four wives, if he treats them equally. This practice is called polygamy. Most Muslim men today choose to marry only one wife.

In India or Pakistan, the bride usually wears a red sari embroidered with gold, in other countries the colours can vary. The groom may be dressed in a simple white robe or in a dark suit. Well-wishers may put colourful garlands round his neck – in India they might be made from sweet-smelling marigolds, roses and jasmine.

▼ *The sisters and mothers of the bride and groom help the bride to dress up in her bridal clothes. They travel with her to the wedding ceremony.*

Islamic religious texts say that to protect her honour, a woman should have her body covered, except for her face and hands. ▶

Apart but together

By tradition, the bride and groom sit on opposite sides of the mosque, or in different rooms. There are two male witnesses to hear their vows and relay them to the other partner. The man leading the wedding may make a speech about the duties of husband and wife and read excerpts from the Qur'an. He asks the bride and groom three times if they consent to the marriage and then pronounces them husband and wife. With their witnesses, they sign the contract they have made.

Bringing gifts

After the ceremony, everyone is given sweetmeats – nuts, dried dates and figs. The bride's relations may feed the groom, and the groom's relations feed the bride, to welcome the couple to their new family. In some cultures, there is a reception given by the bride's parents, to which her friends and relations bring gifts. A week later, the groom hosts his own wedding party, the *walima*, and his side bring their gifts to the couple. In other cultures, there is only one ceremony.

Sacred text

'And among His signs is this, that He created for you mates from among yourselves, that you may dwell in tranquillity with them, and He has put love and mercy between your hearts. Undoubtedly these are signs for those who reflect.'

The Qur'an: 30:21

The Hindu Tradition

▲ In India, preparations for a wedding may involve washing in a holy river such as the Ganges. This purifies and blesses all those taking part in the ceremony.

Parents often advise their children on whom to marry, and consult a priest who reads the couple's horoscopes to see if they are well-suited. But many Hindus choose their own partners. Then their families – especially the senior, or older, ladies in the families – take over the arrangements for the wedding. First, the engagement is announced, and the men of both families meet for prayers and a meal at which they can get to know one another.

A splendid occasion

Because a Hindu wedding is often a huge event, the bride and groom have many preparations to make. The bride often has to choose several outfits for her wedding day. It takes hours to paint the bride's hands and feet with henna patterns and dress her in the red and gold sari and gold jewellery that she will wear at the ceremony. Bride and groom both wear garlands of flowers at the wedding ceremony.

Padmini's story

'My name is Padmini and I live in Canada. At my wedding feast we sat on carpets in a wonderful garden and ate curry with flakes of real gold in it to wish us good fortune. Twenty chefs worked in two tents set up as kitchens to feed all our guests. The wedding lasted for hours and I saw so many people, all of whom came up to wish me well. At the end of the day I was very tired.'

The groom travels to the ceremony on horseback with a parade of family and friends dancing and singing behind him. ▶

A sacred place

A Hindu wedding often lasts all day, and there may be hundreds of guests, so the event often takes place in a hall, or in India, in a special wedding garden. In the middle of the hall, the bride's family set up a sacred place covered with a richly decorated canopy and festooned with flowers. The bride is the first to arrive, but hides out of sight until the bridegroom, usually robed in white, is brought in by his friends. As he enters, lights are waved over his head and grains of rice are thrown to ward off evil. He is also given honey, to sweeten his welcome. Then the bride is brought out to greet him, and their close friends and family cluster round to listen to the ceremony.

The ceremony

The bride pushes back her veil and sits with the groom in front of a sacred fire. The priest sprinkles holy water on the pair and ties their right hands together, asking for blessings from the gods. There are prayers and readings and the bride and groom throw symbolic offerings of food into the fire. The bride places her foot on a stone, as a promise that she will stand firm as a rock to support her husband.

▼ *The bride and groom give each other garlands to wear to signify that they accept one another.*

The seven steps

The most important part of the ceremony is the seven steps. The priest ties the end of the bride's sari to the groom's scarf to show that they are now joined together. They walk seven times round the sacred fire, making a wish for food, strength, wealth, happiness, children, good times together and friendship. Now they are married, and the guests throw flower petals over the couple and give them presents. Sometimes, if the ceremony has been in a public hall, the bride and groom may go to a Hindu temple for a blessing.

Sacred text

'My bride, follow me in my vows. Take the first step for food, take the second step for strength, the third for increasing prosperity, the fourth for happiness, the fifth for children. May we have healthy and long-lived sons. Take the sixth step for seasonal pleasures, take the seventh step for friendship.'

Ashwalayana Grihya Sutra:
The Marriage Mantra

▲ *At this Hindu wedding in Bali, the bride and groom wear ornate gold ornaments and headdresses that are very different to the wedding clothes of Indian Hindus and reflect Balinese culture.*

The new home

Though the ceremony is a long one, it is quite informal, and the guests may talk, laugh and even sing among themselves while it is going on. Afterwards there is a lavish feast with many courses, and then the bride is taken in procession to her new home, where she is carried over the threshold. In countries such as India the bride may move in to live with her husband's family. Hindu households can be very large, with many branches of the same family living under one roof.

The Buddhist Tradition

The Buddha taught about spiritual enlightenment, rather than social arrangements like marriage. So for Buddhists, marriage is not a holy rite but a social contract. A Buddhist wedding may be blessed by a monk or a priest, but what happens during the ceremony varies greatly from one country to the next.

Japanese weddings

In Japan, many Buddhist couples choose to have a Western-style wedding, with a white dress and a tiered cake. This may take place in a hotel in front of a small shrine with a statue, candles and flowers, and an offering of incense. After the wedding, there may be an extravagant party, with music and laser lights and then a honeymoon in a foreign country.

▼ At this Buddhist wedding in Japan the bride wears a kimono, the traditional dress of Japan.

Toshimoto's story

'My name is Toshimoto. I and my bride Yukiko dressed in traditional kimonos for our wedding. The ceremony was held at a Shinto shrine in a Tokyo hotel. We drank a rice wine called saké and I read out the words of commitment. All of our friends were there to witness our joining together. As Buddhists, we believe that the love within a marriage should be pure and without spite. It must not stand in the way of enlightenment by turning to jealousy or deceit.'

▲ *This wedding took place in a refugee camp in Mae Hong Son province, Thailand. The bride's attendants carry gifts of sweets and flowers to place at the shrine to Buddha.*

The sacred scroll

Many Buddhist weddings all over the world take place in the home of the bride. Before the ceremony, the chanting of mantras (sacred words repeated again and again) greets the guests, who are shown to their places by girls wearing white. Then the bride and groom arrive, and are taken by a lay leader (a Buddhist who is not a priest) to a holy cabinet containing a sacred scroll. They kneel in front of the cabinet and perform a short ceremony called *Gong-yo*. This involves reciting *sutras* (wise sayings in Sanskrit, an ancient Indian language) and chanting.

Growing together

Sometimes a Buddhist bride and groom stand or kneel on a special platform, called a *purowa*. Their right hands are tied together with a silk scarf, or they wear bands of silk around their heads, like halos, connected by a silken thread. This shows how their minds will be united in marriage. The pair sip three times from three bowls, first a small bowl, then a bigger bowl, then a third bowl that is bigger still, to symbolize the way their lives will grow together.

▼ *This wedding feast in China was so big that it took place outside. The wedding feast is the part of the wedding where the bride and groom can meet their guests and talk with them.*

◄ *When the couple leave the wedding ceremony, they may have their photographs taken and then go on to the wedding reception.*

Flowers and rings

The bride and groom often make an offering of flowers to the Buddha, whose teachings they will try to follow all their lives. Then they may exchange rings. The person conducting the ceremony will probably make a short speech about the meaning of marriage, and when it is over, the guests all clap and cheer, to wish the couple happiness and good luck. Afterwards, everyone is invited to a wedding feast which might be at somebody's home, in a hall or restaurant.

Friends and supporters

Buddhist couples often choose one or two close friends of their own sex to be sponsors or supporters during their wedding. Like the bride and groom, they may dress in traditional colourful silk wraps with sashes, or in smart Western clothes.

Sacred text

'The support of father and mother, the cherishing of wife and children, and peaceful occupations – this is the Highest Blessing.'

The Maha-Mangala Sutta: Verse 5 (Buddhist Chant)

The Sikh Tradition

◀ *The preparations for the wedding* langar, *the traditional meal that is taken in the community kitchen, take a long time and require a lot of help from family and friends.*

Sikh marriages are usually 'assisted'. This means that families introduce their children to people they think might make good partners for them – but the young people always have the right to say no to their parents' choice. Once the young people are agreed and their families satisfied, wedding plans can go ahead.

Engagement

Before the wedding day, an engagement ceremony takes place at the *gurdwara* (Sikh temple) or at the bride or groom's home. The couple give each other rings and sweetmeats (small cakes and sweets), and the groom is often presented with a *kara* (bracelet) and *kirpan* (dagger), important symbols of the Sikh faith which he will wear at the wedding.

Sita's story

'My name is Sita. My grandpa is a *granthi* – a respected member of the community. He looks after the *Guru Granth Sahib*. This is our holy book. It is kept on a throne under a canopy, and covered at night with rich fabrics. When grandpa reads it, he waves a sacred whisk called a *chauri* above it. Everyone must be barefoot and cover their heads when they are near the holy book.'

A groom on horseback

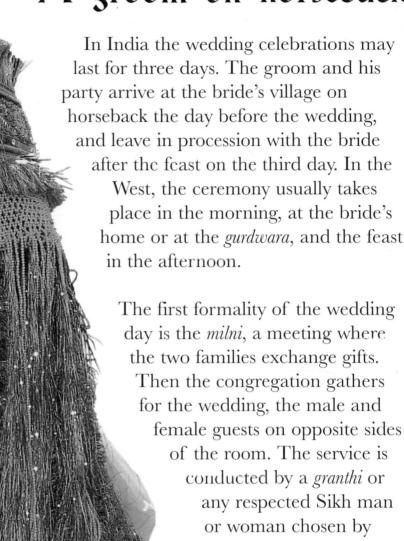

▼ *The groom wears a crown, or sehra, with gilded strings hanging in front of his face.*

In India the wedding celebrations may last for three days. The groom and his party arrive at the bride's village on horseback the day before the wedding, and leave in procession with the bride after the feast on the third day. In the West, the ceremony usually takes place in the morning, at the bride's home or at the *gurdwara*, and the feast in the afternoon.

The first formality of the wedding day is the *milni*, a meeting where the two families exchange gifts. Then the congregation gathers for the wedding, the male and female guests on opposite sides of the room. The service is conducted by a *granthi* or any respected Sikh man or woman chosen by the family.

▲ *When the bride and groom bow in front of the* Guru Granth Sahib *they officially agree to the marriage. Then the bride's father places a garland of flowers on the sacred book.*

Joined by a scarf

The bride wears a kind of trouser suit – a *kameez* and *shalwar* in red, pink or orange; the groom is usually in his best clothes. The couple sit together in front of the *Guru Granth Sahib*, the sacred book. There are hymns and prayers and a short talk about the meaning of marriage. Then the bride's father places one end of the groom's *pulla* (scarf) in his hand and the other in his daughter's hand. Thus joined, the pair take their vows.

The Lavan

Next comes the most important part of the ceremony, the *Lavan* or wedding hymn, which is read from the *Guru Granth Sahib*. With each of the four verses, the groom leads the bride in a circle around the holy book. After the fourth circle, the couple are married, and the guests shower them with rose petals. A final prayer and reading, then *parshad*, a sweet dish made with flour, butter and sugar, is served to the congregation.

Sacred text

'In this first circle, God has shown you the duties of family life. Accept the Guru's word as your guide and it will make you free from sin. Meditate on the Name of God, which is the theme of all the scriptures. Devote yourself to God and all evil will go away. Blessed are those who hold God in their hearts. They are always content and happy.'

The Lavan: Verse 1

Farewell

After the ceremony, well-wishers often give money to the newly married couple, and coconuts for good luck. These are not religious ceremonies; they are cultural. When the wedding feast is over, the groom accompanies his bride back to his home, which will now be her home too. In a gesture of farewell and good wishes, she throws a handful of rice over her shoulder to those who are left behind at the feast.

▼ *The groom gives thanks for the money and presents that his guests have given to him and his bride by bowing before the gifts.*

GLOSSARY

Allah the Muslim name for one God.

Ark a cupboard in a synagogue in which the *Torah* is kept.

banns these are called in church three times, to ask the congregation if they know of any reason why a couple should not marry (such as, that they are already married).

bedecken a tradition in which a Jewish groom lifts his bride's veil to identify her.

best man a friend of the groom, who supports him at his Christian wedding.

Bible the holy book of the Christians.

bridesmaid a friend of the bride, who supports her at her Christian wedding.

Catholicism the Roman Catholic Church headed by the Pope.

chauri a whisk waved above the Sikh holy book during readings.

church a Christian place of worship.

confetti tiny pieces of coloured paper, thrown over the bride and groom at a wedding.

engagement a promise or commitment to marry.

Gong-yo a Buddhist religious ceremony.

granthi a Sikh priest.

Guru Granth Sahib the Sikh holy book.

gurdwara the Sikh place of worship.

henna a herb that dyes skin and hair red.

honeymoon a holiday that begins married life in many religions.

huppah the canopy under which Jews get married.

imam a Muslim priest.

kara a bracelet worn by Sikh men and women.

kirpan a dagger carried by Sikh men and women.

Lavan a Sikh wedding hymn.

mehndi a paste made with henna for decorating the hands and feet.

mikveh the Jewish purification pool.

milni the meeting before a Sikh wedding of the two families.

minyan a group of at least ten adult men who witness a Jewish wedding.

mosque the Muslim place of worship.

Orthodox a traditional way of life or belief.

parshad a sweetmeat traditionally eaten at a Sikh wedding.

polygamy the practice of taking more than one wife.

Prophet Muhammad (Peace Be Upon Him) a Muslim chosen by Allah to teach God's message. The words in brackets are the standard phrase repeated after the name of Islamic prophets is used.

Protestantism the religion established in protest against Catholicism.

pulla the scarf worn by a groom at a Sikh wedding.

purowa a platform on which Buddhists may get married.

Qur'an Muslim holy book.

rabbi a Jewish priest.

register office a building where legal contracts of marriage are made.

synagogue the Jewish place of worship.

Torah the holy book of the Jews.

FURTHER INFORMATION

Books

Beliefs and Cultures: Christian by Carol Watson, Watts, 1996.

The Jewish World by Douglas Charing, Simon and Schuster Young Books, 1992.

Islam (World Religions) by Khadijah Knight, Wayland, 1995.

Islam (World Religions) by Richard Tames, Watts, 1999.

What do we know about Buddhism? by Anita Ganeri, Macdonald Young Books, 1997.

Hinduism (World Religions) by Katherine Prior, Watts, 1999.

What do we know about Hinduism? by Anita Ganeri, Macdonald Young Books, 1995

Sikhism (World Religions) by Kanwaljit Kaur-Singh, Wayland, 1995.

What I Believe (Discover the Religions of the World) by Alan Brown and Andrew Langley, Macdonald Young Books, 1999.

Websites

education@clear-vision.org – The website for the Clear Vision Trust, a project that provides Buddhist resources.

http://www.sikhfoundation.org/ – The Sikh Foundation.

http://www.hindusamajtemple.org/ht/hindu.html – An introduction to Hinduism.

http://www.islamicity.org/ – An introduction to the world of Islam.

http://conline.net/ – Christians Online, a Christian resource.

http://www.jewishweb.com/ – The Worldwide Jewish Web.

INDEX

All the numbers in **bold** refer to photographs